Straight from the Heart

Straight from the Heart

Reflections from Twentieth-Century Mystics

Edited by
DICK RYAN

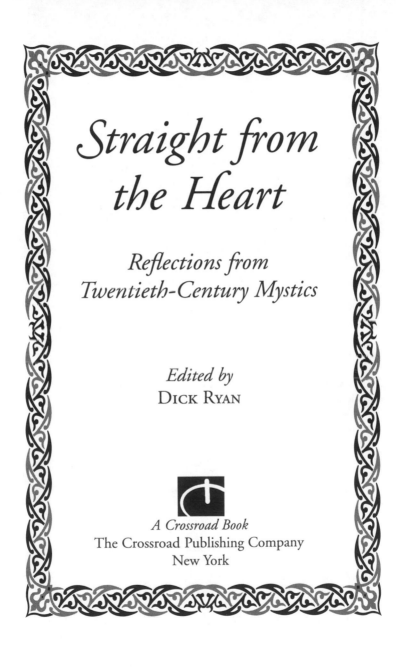

A Crossroad Book
The Crossroad Publishing Company
New York

The Crossroad Publishing Company
481 Eighth Avenue, New York, NY 10001

Printed in the United States of America

Library of Congress Cataloging-in-Publication Data

Straight from the heart : reflections from 20th century mystics / edited by Dick Ryan.
    p. cm.
  ISBN 0-8245-1923-X
   1. Devotional calendars. 2. Christian life—Quotations, maxims, etc. I. Ryan, Dick.
  BV4810 .S84115 2001
  242'.2—dc21

                            2001002473

1 2 3 4 5 6 7 8 9 10 05 04 03 02 01

Contents

Foreword • vii

Charity • 1

Commitment • 11

Community • 15

Compassion • 27

Conversion • 39

Death • 43

Faith • 47

Forgiveness • 55

Freedom • 65

Gratitude • 74

Contents

Healing • 77

Hope • 84

Humility • 94

Intimacy • 102

Justice • 108

Ministry • 115

Passion • 121

Prayer • 128

Solitude • 137

Spirituality • 145

Suffering • 156

Vocation • 169

Acknowledgments • 179

Foreword

When we think of mystics, we usually think of people from the past who have contributed to the spiritual energy of the world through their close communion with God—people such as St. Teresa of Avila and Meister Eckhart. Rarely do we appreciate the mystics who live among us here and now.

Through their writings, these modern mystics demonstrate their profound reverence for both the past and the present. In revealing their own experiences of life before their God, they allow us a glimpse of their own hearts, the heart of the divine, and hopefully our own hearts as well.

It was this impact that made the task of editing the work so inspiring and so different from editing any other book. Whether you start with the theme of commitment or that of humility—and make your own decision about where you wish to start your journey—the meditations will take you out of your own ambit and show you life with a new perspective. This in itself is a gift of divine proportions.

It is not possible to capture every profound insight of all the mystics, let alone of those we have sampled within these pages. This would be the task of a documented history if an editor were to attempt such an undertaking. The pages that follow are

Foreword

to be pondered and reflected upon until the words and their meanings become embedded in our own hearts and then lived and breathed as part of our own lives.

DICK RYAN
Editor

Charity

Our faithfulness will depend on our willingness to go where there is brokenness, loneliness, and human need. If the church has a future it is a future with the poor in whatever form.

HENRI J. M. NOUWEN
Sabbatical Journey

Charity

*riendship more than any other experience is
essential for moral health. Call to mind someone who lacks healthy friendships, and I guarantee
that you have identified someone with poor moral
health.*

CHARLES M. SHELTON
Achieving Moral Health

&

*he deepest wisdom man can attain is to
know that his destiny is to aid, to serve.*

ABRAHAM JOSHUA HESCHEL
I Asked for Wonder

Charity

If anyone thinks that you can stop giving in the meantime, then he has parted company with all Christian morality.

C. S. LEWIS
The Joyful Christian

&

The priority of charity in the Christian moral life gives us the key to all the other obligations of a Christian.

THOMAS MERTON
Life and Holiness

Charity

The ability to respect the outsider is probably the litmus test of true seeing. . . . One God, one world, one truth, one suffering, and one love. All we can do is participate.

RICHARD ROHR
Everything Belongs

&

If being involved in others' failures through love and caring brings us personal suffering, so be it. We follow a crucified God, who truly suffered for love rather than retreat to the power of unmoved self-sufficiency and detachment.

SIDNEY CALLAHAN
With All Our Heart and Mind

Charity

he call to holiness means nothing else but the call to compassionate, sympathetic and active love of one's neighbor in accord with the ideal and the example of God.

BERNARD HÄRING
What Does Christ Want?

&

he thing about life that so many persons do not suspect is that it gives us something only if we are always giving something of ourselves first.

EUGENE KENNEDY
Free To Be Human

Charity

Charity is impossible without an interior poverty of spirit which identifies us with the unfortunate, the underprivileged, the dispossessed.

THOMAS MERTON
Life and Holiness

&

Our passionate concern for the masses must find incarnate experience in helping our neighbors, and we need not have to ask who they are.

ROBERT F. MORNEAU
Ashes to Easter

Charity

*A*ctive, loving concern for the temporal well-being and the eternal salvation of our fellow man is the most fitting expression of true worship of God.

BERNARD HÄRING
What Does Christ Want?

&

*J*esus invites us to dine at the table of sinners, to seek out and save the stray, to embrace the orphan and widow. Since God is love we must look for the deity in the land of charity.

ROBERT F. MORNEAU
Ashes to Easter

Charity

Our struggle will not be to evangelize in the sense of proselytizing but to evangelize in the sense of the example we set by bringing love everywhere. Our work will be to feed the hungry, to clothe the naked, to shelter the shelterless, to visit the imprisoned. That will be the essence of evangelization.

DAVID RICHO
Catholic Means Universal

&

Knowing one's self, finding one's self, and expending one's self for another are intertwined activities. Love of self, love of God, and love of neighbor are interdependent.

SIDNEY CALLAHAN
With All Our Heart and Mind

8

Charity

I t is sad to see that, in our highly competitive and greedy world, we have lost touch with th joy of giving. We often live as if our happiness depended on having. But I don't know anyone who is really happy because of what he or she has. True joy, happiness and inner peace come from the giving of ourselves to others. A happy life is a life for others.

HENRI J. M. NOUWEN
Life of the Beloved

Charity

We cross new hurdles every time our own spiritual growth serves the good of others. Such is the case when we practice social justice, peace and mercy; when we show compassion for our own and others' vulnerability; when we make Christ the center of our life while reaching out to others in his name.

SUSAN MUTO
Late Have I Loved Thee

Commitment

ur fundamental challenge is not fidelity to our commitments, but fidelity to the truth. It is this fidelity that discerns and actualizes our commitment to God in the heart of our finite choices and which, finally, justifies our relative commitments and strengthens us to live them in hope.

SANDRA M. SCHNEIDERS
Written That You May Believe

Commitment

We best understand the link between our human actions and their moral significance when examining the two commitments that provide our lives their most valued meaning: working and loving.

CHARLES M. SHELTON
Achieving Moral Health

Commitment

A Christian is committed to the belief that Love and Mercy are the most powerful forces on earth.

THOMAS MERTON
Passion for Peace

&

Resolutions don't usually work. There has to be a deeper commitment than that. We have to take a stand and make a declaration: I am a person who meets the Lord each day as a friend and disciple, sitting at his feet to receive a word of life.

M. BASIL PENNINGTON
Lectio Divina

Commitment

To keep on keeping on, to persevere, renews hope and strengthens our commitments. Fidelity deepens the bond.

SIDNEY CALLAHAN
With All Our Heart and Mind

&

To be adult in faith is to make a commitment to a message that challenges us to love with all our heart no matter what . . . to let love reach its full stature in our every thought, word, and deed.

DAVID RICHO
Catholic Means Universal

Community

*he Christian love which is the basis of
community therefore also includes the necessity to recognize the need for deep involvement in
present-day work of political, cultural and social
emancipation.*

EDWARD SCHILLEBEECKX
Church

Community

The forms that our lives take — our family, our schools, our churches, our society — are all unconscious, preconceived hand-me-downs. This is our reality; this is the realm in which we struggle, in which we are failures or successes.

STEVEN HARRISON
Being One

&

When a person is on a serious inner journey to his or her own powerlessness, and meanwhile is in immediate contact with the powerless men and women of the world, then community will result.

RICHARD ROHR
Simplicity

hile community ritual is one way God's presence is expressed in worship, the community itself often becomes the presence of God for us.

DEBRA K. FARRINGTON
Romancing the Holy

&

he Church will not cease to teach and stress the fact that the family is the fundamental community, where man can and should learn the true meaning of love and the spirit of responsibility.

BERNARD HÄRING
What Does Christ Want?

Community

he community is always there, irritating and demanding as it can be, constantly prodding you to leave selfishness behind, constantly nourishing your soul in ways you would never think of on your own.

MITCH FINLEY
101 Ways to Nourish Your Soul

&

he task of the community is to be, through love, Jesus' bodily presence, and thus the giver of his Spirit, to all who come to believe down through the ages.

SANDRA M. SCHNEIDERS
Written That You May Believe

Community

As church we are called to tell the story of Jesus, recall his dangerous memory, walk in his footsteps and, in the power of the Spirit, struggle against the forces of death.

ELIZABETH A. JOHNSON
Consider Jesus

&

The life of communion is more than just an imitation of Christ. When we engage in the life of communion, when we move beyond ourselves to attend to the world around us in an event of communion, when we orient ourselves to the needs and concerns of others, we are being drawn by the Holy Spirit into the divine life of God.

RICHARD R. GAILLARDETZ
Transforming Our Days

uilding community is like making a quilt: we all have our own patch; yet a common thread unites us.

JAMES CONLON
The Sacred Impulse

&

he church has to do with a unique relation-ship of communion with God that we have as a people: a relationship that, if properly understood, is a love relationship quite capable of evoking senti-ments of love and endearment, such as any couple in love might experience.

WILLIAM SHANNON
Silence on Fire

ince peace and justice are among the most powerful signs of the reign of God present in this world, it belongs to the essential mission of the church to make these realities more visible in our time.

ELIZABETH A. JOHNSON
Consider Jesus

Community

ommunity can only exist in the tension between solitude and togetherness. The delicate balance between solitude and togetherness will determine what kind of community it shall be. In the togetherness community of which married life is the prototype, togetherness is the measure of solitude: each of the partners must have as much solitude as they need for rich and full togetherness.

BROTHER DAVID STEINDL-RAST
A Listening Heart

I am discovering that I am more, not less, a Catholic, when I am willing to recognize all the things that God is doing outside the parameters of the institutional structure of which I am, by choice, a part.

WILLIAM SHANNON
Silence on Fire

Community

hen we stand in awe of the wonders of God's creation, when we find ourselves grasped by a piece of music or a beautiful painting, we experience a kind of self-forgetfulness that draws us beyond ourselves into communion with our larger world.

RICHARD R. GAILLARDETZ
Transforming Our Days

&

e can read, pray, and study in solitude sometimes — even often. But we miss out on something valuable, and we fail to see the full face of God, when we choose to search, all alone, for God.

DEBRA K. FARRINGTON
Romancing the Holy

Community

*T*he love we give each other
Is that which builds us up.
We live in one another;
We share a common cup.
Our loves are each a whisper
Of one sweet voice divine,
And when we sing together
The chorus is sublime.
—Haskell Miller

PHYLLIS TICKLE (ED.)
The Divine Hours

Community

I n entering a community, the individual sets
himself the task of living above his own
ordinary level, and thus perfecting his own being,
living more fully, by his efforts to live for the benefit
of others besides himself.

THOMAS MERTON
The Silent Life

&

N ot only does all fatherhood and motherhood
come from God, but also all friendship,
partnership in marriage, and true intimacy
and community.

HENRI J. M. NOUWEN
Here and Now

Compassion

Compassion is not nodding "yes, yes" behind the daily paper while someone stands in front of us trying to have their heart heard.

JOAN CHITTISTER
The Psalms

Compassion

od had to get dirty. This sinking into the dirt — this divine solidarity with the lost — is the "sacrifice" which the Son makes to the infinite pleasure of the Father. It is a sacrifice expressive, not of anger or vengeance, but of compassion.

ROBERT BARRON
Heaven in Stone and Glass

Compassion

he goal is to avoid being so busy carrying inappropriate burdens that we don't have a free hand to carry the burdens that are meant for us. Thus, in being compassionate we are asked to be good stewards of our daily schedule.

ROBERT WICKS
Availability

Compassion

ithout love and compassion for others, our own apparent "love" for Christ is a fiction.

THOMAS MERTON
Life and Holiness

&

ur tears tell us that we are alive, that we have roots in the lives of others, and that we have been touched by the warmest of suns — human love. We should resolve that nobody we love ever has to cry alone.

EUGENE KENNEDY
Free To Be Human

Compassion

God's compassion is not to be confused with Disney World. God does not give us a marshmallow life. God gives us life in all its learnings. God's compassion simply means that God will be there with us in all of them.

JOAN CHITTISTER
The Psalms

Compassion

As we become willing to meet our pain face to face, we need to embrace it with a compassionate heart, to meet it with love and tenderness, no matter how beaten, broken, or unwanted it may seem to us. We need to be as kind with our pain as we would with someone else who is suffering.

JOYCE RUPP
Your Sorrow Is My Sorrow

Compassion

ompassion is one of the fruits of prayer and contemplation. In this encounter with God our whole being is opened up to experience the brokenness of all creation. We find ourselves united not only with God but with all who live.

M. BASIL PENNINGTON
Lectio Divina

&

he whole idea of compassion, which is central to Mahayana Buddhism, is based on a keen awareness of the interdependence of all these living beings, which are all part of one another and all involved in one another.

THOMAS MERTON
The Asian Journal of Thomas Merton

Compassion

here is much grief and pain in our lives, but what a blessing it is when we do not have to live our grief and pain alone. That is the gift of compassion.

HENRI J. M. NOUWEN
Here and Now

&

s long as we live on this earth, our lives as Christians must be marked by compassion. But we must (realize) that the compassionate life is not our final goal. In fact, we can only live the compassionate life to the fullest when we know that it points beyond itself.

HENRI J. M. NOUWEN
Show Me the Way

Compassion

ompassion is not elitist. It is not about pity or "feeling sorry" for others. Its tradition is born out of a shared interdependence and a sense of awe. We live in the fetal waters of cosmic grace. Not only must we celebrate this, but we must struggle for those in our midst who are deeply wounded by poverty of soul and-or body.

JAMES CONLON
The Sacred Impulse

Compassion

"The bowels of mercy" may indeed sound earthy, but it makes very graphic the fact that true compassion rises out of the center of our being: where we are most fully ourselves and most profoundly aware of our oneness with God and with our sisters and brothers.

WILLIAM SHANNON
Silence on Fire

Compassion

I have needed to be compassionate toward myself when I was hurting. I have also needed to offer compassion and kindness to others. One of my best sparks for love and for forgiveness of old relationship hurts came from an image of myself at the Last Supper table, seeing my "enemies" seated next to me, all of us being loved equally by God.

JOYCE RUPP
Dear Heart, Come Home

Compassion

entleness and compassion are the criteria of genuine spirituality. Only when men and women have become gentle and merciful and deal compassionately with their fellow human beings do they bear witness to a spirituality that is in keeping with Christ.

ANSELM GRUEN
Heaven Begins Within You

&

henever we show compassion for our own or others' vulnerability we are soothed with the splendor of intimacy. This gift is given and received every time a parent tucks a tired, tearful child in bed or a caregiver does something to soften the pain. In this spirit-to-spirit exchange, expressed as tender mercy, intimacy is born and compassion flourishes.

SUSAN MUTO
Late Have I Loved Thee

Conversion

*he great commandment is not "thou shalt be
right." The great commandment is to "be in
love." Be inside the great compassion, the great
stream, the great river.*

RICHARD ROHR
Everything Belongs

R eligion consists
of God's question
and man's answer.

ABRAHAM JOSHUA HESCHEL
I Asked for Wonder

&

F aith cannot rest. Faith definitions grow old as
we move through our lives. Periodically we
have to say, "Lord, what does faith mean now?"
This isn't easy.

RICHARD ROHR
Job and the Mystery of Suffering

Conversion

he converted person does not say that nothing matters any more, but that everything that is happens in God and that he is the dwelling place where we come to know the true order of things.

HENRI J. M. NOUWEN
Show Me the Way

&

he human soul has never been as parched with thirst as it is today. And this, I believe, is precisely why we are ready to "go the lengths of God," and can open ourselves up to the healing, conversion, and reconciliation that prayer engenders.

BARBARA FIAND
Prayer and the Quest for Healing

Conversion

his is what conversion is all about. It is a complete turnaround that allows us to discover that we are not the prisoners we think we are.

HENRI J. M. NOUWEN
Here and Now

&

here can be no such thing as instant holiness or instant conversion. It is impossible to love God enough or to reach spiritual perfection in this life. There is no "fast track" to spiritual growth.

DENNIS E. TAMBURELLO
Bernard of Clairvaux

Death

ven those who die victimized, those who disappear, those who are no longer part of the living history of the earth, those no longer remembered — all these people are not beyond the reach of the living God.

ELIZABETH JOHNSON
Consider Jesus

Death

This is the meaning of death: the ultimate self-dedication to the divine. Death so understood will not be distorted by the craving for immortality, for this act of giving away is reciprocity on man's part for God's gift of life.

ABRAHAM JOSHUA HESCHEL
I Asked for Wonder

&

The person discovers in death what was always true, but not adverted to, that we are in God. Death is being in the Hidden Ground of Love in full attentive awareness.

WILLIAM SHANNON
Silence on Fire

Death

onesty demands that we admit our fear, but faith invites us to trust that Jesus walks toward us at every juncture of life. We are not alone now nor will we be at the hour of our death.

ROBERT F. MORNEAU
From Resurrection to Pentecost

&

od did not will Jesus to die. God simply surrendered Jesus to us and our institutions, death-dealing as they are at times. No, what God willed for Jesus was resurrection and that, we too often forget, is precisely what God wills for us. So rise, why don't you?

JOAN CHITTISTER
The Psalms

Death

In the face of death, I realized that it was not love that kept me clinging to life but unresolved anger. Love, real love flowing from me or toward me, sets me free to die.

HENRI J. M. NOUWEN
Beyond the Mirror

&

Mary holding the crucified Jesus is every sorrowing person who embraces a loved one and bids a final farewell. Mary is everyone filled with anguish and sorrow who has held what has died in their life and wondered why it happened.

JOYCE RUPP
Your Sorrow Is My Sorrow

Faith

I f we are to find a faith by which we can live today and a God in whom this generation can have confidence, then we must be willing to be led into the wilderness where our ideas about both God and life can be tested, refined, and remolded. That wilderness will be filled with change, risk, and uncertainty, but there is no alternative open to us except to enter it.

JOHN SHELBY SPONG
The Bishop's Voice

Faith

*P*eople of faith know that God is working with them, through everything that happens to them, to prepare them to become the people they were meant to be. Therefore, they have all the reason in the world to accept themselves for who they are, to accept their past for what it was, and to face their future without fear.

ROBERT J. CORMIER
A Faith That Makes Sense

Faith

ncertainty and belief are a divided world only in thought. In actuality they are the same. Belief cannot exist without uncertainty. Good cannot exist without bad. The saints of the world would be unemployed without sin. . . . They are not two distinct qualities, but rather aspects of the same.

STEVEN HARRISON
Being One

Faith

or those who can imagine the life of faith as a dance with God, it colors our whole spirituality. If we dance with God, it doesn't much matter where we dance. If the divine partner shifts slightly beyond the polished surface of the ballroom, who's complaining? With someone so accomplished, we learn to trust the moves.

KATHY COFFEY
Dancing in the Margins

Faith

God loves us when we cannot;
God holds us when we will not;
God sees us when we dare not;
God knows us when we do not.

EDWINA GATELEY
A Mystical Heart

Faith is a free gift. Each dawn we must again
ask for this grace and resolve to live it as
deeply as possible. With this gift we can venture
into the future assured that God will be faithful to
divine promises and we will experience the fire of
the Spirit enkindling our hearts to burn with
concern for others.

ROBERT F. MORNEAU
From Resurrection to Pentecost

Faith

The Church, which for long has prided itself in surviving so many crises, may at last have to acknowledge that it, too, is temporary in nature. Its task is to serve a larger reality, one that becomes much more coherent and challenging as global horizons expand at many different levels of life. All indications are that this will be a painful transition for all the churches.

DIARMUID O'MURCHÚ
Our World in Transition

Faith

One of the greatest acts of faith is to believe that the few years we live on this earth are like a little seed planted in a very rich soil. For this seed to bear fruit, it must die. We often see or feel only the dying, but the harvest will be abundant even when we ourselves are not the harvesters.

HENRI J. M. NOUWEN
Life of the Beloved

Faith

I do not need
To pursue God.
I do not need
To chant and cry aloud.
I do not need
To seek out holy places,
Blessed shrines
And holy signs.
I need only,
O God,
I need only
To whisper —
Yes.

EDWINA GATELEY
A Mystical Heart

Forgiveness

For me, the utter powerlessness of God is that God forgives. I hold myself in a position of power by not forgiving myself or others. God does not hold on to that position of power.

RICHARD ROHR
Everything Belongs

orgiveness is not easy. It is clearly a gift. It is a grace for which we must earnestly wait and pray, even if the waiting can be excruciating at times. For a while we may find ourselves having to forgive ourselves for not being able to forgive, for not wanting to forgive, or for not wanting even to pray for the grace to want to forgive.

BARBARA FIAND
Prayer and the Quest for Healing

Forgiveness

A marvelous freedom comes to us when we possess courage enough to see ourselves pretty much as we are. This freedom gives us the capacity to forgive others, a moral authority that springs from the love itself, the love that comes into life when we are truly in touch with the persons we are.

EUGENE KENNEDY
The Pain of Being Human

he essential sacrament of reconciliation has always been sincerity and contrition as one approaches Eucharist and touches the Christian community.

RONALD ROLHEISER
The Holy Longing

&

nce we are able to forgive, we can be grateful for what we have received. And we have received so much.

HENRI J. M. NOUWEN
Here and Now

Forgiveness

orgiveness is neither soft-hearted nor soft-
headed; it is tough and unblinking realistic
when it is rooted in an accurate understanding of
what can go on between us and others.

EUGENE KENNEDY
A Sense of Life, A Sense of Sin

&

o forgive our enemies doesn't lie within our
power. That is a divine gift. That's why it's so
important to make the Eucharist the heart and
center of your life. It's there that you receive the
love that empowers you to take the way that Jesus
has taken before you.

HENRI J. M. NOUWEN
Show Me the Way

Forgiveness

Forgiving all injuries is so completely against our human nature that we give up in despair and recognize that we are unable to do it by ourselves. We simply can't do it without God.

SIDNEY CALLAHAN
With All Our Heart and Mind

Forgiveness has nothing to do with logic. It is the final breakdown of logic.

RICHARD ROHR
Everything Belongs

Forgiveness

he final and sharpest test of redeemed love is love of one's enemies, the strength and firmness of love precisely at the point where we meet resistance, misunderstanding, rejection and contempt.

BERNARD HÄRING
What Does Christ Want?

&

orgiveness is moving on. It is freeing up and putting to better use the energy once consumed by holding grudges and harboring resentments. It is recognizing that we have better things to do with our lives and then doing them.

PETER M. KALELLIS
Restoring Relationships

Forgiveness

orgiveness is not about accepting someone else's humanity. It is much harder; it is about accepting our own humanity. It is about accepting God's design of us rather than our own. It is about believing in ourselves by virtue of our own decision and not because of the opinion of any other person.

ROBERT J. CORMIER
A Faith That Makes Sense

Forgiveness

Very often in our discussions around the topic of forgiveness we revert to the slogan "forgive and forget." Nothing hinders the healing process more. Perhaps the exhortation "Remember — and pray for the grace to forgive and be forgiven" is more realistic.

BARBARA FIAND
Prayer and the Quest for Healing

Forgiveness

Maybe the reason it seems hard for me to forgive others is that I do not fully believe that I am a forgiven person. If I could fully accept the truth that I am forgiven and do not have to live in guilt or shame, I would really be free.

HENRI J. M. NOUWEN
Show Me the Way

&

The world craves for the energy of helpers who fail but who can succeed in remembering that they are forgiven and can attempt to model this important Christian reality for others.

ROBERT WICKS
Availability

Freedom

We are free human beings because nothing in this world can control the divine core within us. Nothing can reach and manipulate the very center of our being where God dwells within us.

ANSELM GRUEN
Building Self-Esteem

The Church ought to provide its people with
skills in making decisions instead of trying to
take away their freedom and force them all to do
exactly what the letter of the law demands.

ANDREW GREELEY
Windows

&

Only when we rest in God can we find the
safety, the spaciousness, and the scary freedom
to be who we are, all that we are, more than we
are, and less than we are.

RICHARD ROHR
Everything Belongs

Freedom

*J*esus wants to set us free, free from everything that prevents us from fully following our vocation, free also from everyone who prevents us from fully knowing God's unconditional love.

HENRI J. M. NOUWEN
Here and Now

&

*S*ecular freedom is having to do what you want to do. Religious freedom is wanting to do what you have to do.

RICHARD ROHR
Everything Belongs

Freedom

nner freedom means that no one can have power over my inner self. This inner freedom gives me independence even in friendship. I do not define myself in other people's terms. I am always myself. Such freedom is necessary for friendship or marriage to succeed.

ANSELM GRUEN
Angels of Grace

hen we truly learn to trust God's presence in every moment of our lives, we no longer need to control our outcomes. We are set free, as it were. We can let go and find peace. We accept the harmony and the oneness of it all.

BARBARA FIAND
Prayer and the Quest for Healing

Freedom

 reedom is hard to come by. We cling to old
 patterns of thought; we get into ruts that
imprison us in comforting behavior; we retain
habits of the heart that contract rather than expand
our love. Jesus comes to set us free by teaching us to
do all that the Father taught him.

ROBERT F. MORNEAU
Ashes to Easter

Freedom

ternal death is as possible as eternal life! God offers us a choice. To say yes or no to love. To offer me a choice is to respect me as a free human person. I am no robot or automaton who has no choice. God, who loves me in freedom, wants my love in freedom. That means that no is a possibility. Eternal life is not a predetermined fact. It is the fruit of our human response.

HENRI J. M. NOUWEN
Sabbatical Journey

Freedom

*A*ll the things that season our character —
and trust, friendship and faithfulness —
must come freely through the medium of time or
they do not come at all.

EUGENE KENNEDY
The Pain of Being Human

&

*C*ommunity requires the breath and breadth of
freedom. Solitude and community must be in
healthy tension. If the community becomes absolute,
we crowd each other so much we can hardly
breathe. The community will only be fruitful when
each of us in the community can also go our own
particular personal inner way.

ANSELM GRUEN
Angels of Grace

Freedom

uiet, quiet — that wonderful freedom to be
able to rest quietly in the Lord, knowing that
in him we have all. No longer tugged this way and
that by our passions, emotions, uncontrolled desires
— this is what was behind all the austerity of the
desert, what motivated it, and what encouraged
the monks and nuns to persevere in it.

M. BASIL PENNINGTON
Lectio Divina

Freedom

A Christianity that cannot engage the knowledge of the world in which it lives, that shouts its creedal affirmations defiantly as if they are self-evidently true, that believes the articulations of its faith convictions are unchanging and infallible, is a Christianity that will surely die.

JOHN SHELBY SPONG
The Bishop's Voice

The theology of baptism tells us that we died to this world together with Christ when we were baptized. In this context, dying to the world has no negative implications but means taking the way of freedom. If I am dead to this world, it has no power over me.

ANSELM GRUEN
Building Self-Esteem

Gratitude

A life of faith is a life of gratitude — it means a life in which I am willing to experience my complete dependence upon God and to praise and thank him unceasingly for the gift of being.

HENRI J. M. NOUWEN
Show Me the Way

Gratitude

*T*o be a presence of perpetual thanksgiving may be the ultimate goal of life. The thankful person is the one for whom life is simply one long exercise in the sacred.

JOAN CHITTISTER
The Psalms

&

*O*nly one response can maintain us: gratefulness for witnessing the wonder, for the gift of our unearned right to serve, to adore, and to fulfill. It is gratefulness which makes the soul great.

ABRAHAM JOSHUA HESCHEL
I Asked for Wonder

Gratitude

rue spiritual gratitude embraces all of our past, the good as well as the bad events, the joyful as well as the sorrowful. From the place where we stand, everything that took place took us to this place, and we want to remember all of it as part of God's guidance.

HENRI J. M. NOUWEN
Here and Now

Healing

Christian nonviolence is not built on a presupposed division, but on the basic unity of man. It is not out for the conversion of the wicked to the ideas of the good, but for the healing and reconciliation of man with himself, man the person and man the human family.

THOMAS MERTON
Passion for Peace

Healing

ealing begins when, in the face of our own
darkness, we recognize our helplessness and
surrender our need for control . . . we face what is,
and we ask for mercy.

BARBARA FIAND
Prayer and the Quest for Healing

&

ouch heals. . . . Touch keeps blessing in flow.
The more alert we become to the blessing that
flows into us through everything we touch, the more
our own touch will bring blessing.

BROTHER DAVID STEINDL-RAST
A Listening Heart

Healing

To believe in Jesus as the Christ means at its deepest to confess and at the same time to recognize that Jesus has an abiding and constitutive significance for the approach of the kingdom of God and thus for the comprehensive healing of human beings and making them whole.

EDWARD SCHILLEBEECKX
Church

Healing

No matter what we name it, the struggle is always an attempt to make sense of our lives. Whether the foil of the moment is the church, the boss, the sibling, the spouse, we are always cast back on the same old self and inner resources. Whatever the particular struggle, the soul needs the same nurture: tenderness, compassion, meaning, the abiding presence of God.

KATHY COFFEY
Dancing in the Margins

Healing

I have learned many things about woundedness and healing. These images have helped me to see how essential it is to let go of old wounds in order to be healed and to stop trying to control everything, or to figure it all out, or to make it go a certain way.

JOYCE RUPP
Dear Heart, Come Home

To be able to accept myself as being wounded, as truly in solidarity with broken humanity and in need of forgiveness and healing, is already grace and is, in itself in fact, the first dimension of healing.

BARBARA FIAND
Prayer and the Quest for Healing

81

Healing

It is through the process of healing that we become more accepting of ourselves and less fearful of who we are. When we bid farewell to our wounds, we regain the inner energy that has been focused on the hurt. It is often through facing our struggles and painful ordeals that we discover greater clarity and learn what gives our life direction and meaning.

JOYCE RUPP
Dear Heart, Come Home

Healing

Could you help me
This afternoon to heal
To lay hands on to heal?
I stared at Jesus
Had not told him
Anything about myself
What could I say?
Of course I will help you
Powerful strong like the sun
Jesus reaching over.

MICHAEL KENNEDY
Eyes on Jesus

Hope

Why should we worry about anything? Tumors? Cancer? Death? Why not rather turn to God, whose solicitude for our individual welfare — temporally as well as spiritually — puts all created solicitude out of the picture.

MICHAEL CROSBY (EDITOR)
Solanus Casey

Hope

ope is not just one single quality or promise.
Hope has to do with believing beyond today
— knowing there's a garden of beauty that awaits
me. Hope encourages me to follow my dreams,
to believe in the part of me that envisions my
wholeness.

JOYCE RUPP
Dear Heart, Come Home

&

here is an intimate relationship between joy
and hope. While optimism makes us live as if
someday soon things will go better for us, hope frees
us from the need to predict the future and allows us
to live in the present, with the deep trust that God
will never leave us alone but will fulfill the deepest
desires of our heart.

HENRI J. M. NOUWEN
Here and Now

Hope

H ope is a virtue for every season and every
trial of our existence, the one source of energy
and purpose that is strong enough for the way life
really is.

EUGENE KENNEDY
Free To Be Human

&

I f our hope is based only on what we can do
and what we can change, in the end our efforts
won't mean much to others.

ROBERT WICKS
Availability

Hope

*T*he story of the resurrection in Matthew wants
to awaken our trust that the state of the grave
does not remain permanent for children or adults.
When everything is dark and full of sadness and life
is covered in depression, an angel comes down from
heaven and causes an earthquake.

ANSELM GRUEN
Everybody Has an Angel

Hope

I f we are on the brink of a new evolutionary threshold, not even the churches will survive in the old mould; they, too, will fade into oblivion. And the Kingdom — if it is to survive, and I for one, believe it will — will thrive outside rather than within the institutional churches.

DIARMUID O'MURCHÚ
Our World in Transition

Hope

People of hope live in the world but not of it,
   detached from both its pleasures and tragedies,
always looking toward the will and work of God.
The Christian icon of hope is the cross.

ROBERT BARRON
Heaven in Stone and Glass

&

Poverty, pain, struggle, anguish, agony, and even
   inner darkness may continue to be part of our
existence. They may even be God's way of purifying
us. But life is no longer boring, resentful, depress-
ing, or lonely because we have come to know that
everything that happens is part of our way to the
house of the Father.

HENRI J. M. NOUWEN
Show Me the Way

Hope

In the midst of sorrow, human beings stretch to touch a thimbleful of hope.
In the turmoil and struggle of brutal loss, the human heart pleads for some sense amid senselessness.
In the emptiness of pain, the human spirit longs for a glimmer of love.

JOYCE RUPP
Your Sorrow Is My Sorrow

&

Leaving behind the ones you love, the flowers and the trees, the mountains and the oceans, the beauty of art and music, and all the exuberant gifts of life cannot be just the destruction and cruel end of all things; then indeed we have to wait for the third day.

HENRI J. M. NOUWEN
Show Me the Way

Hope

The problem is that we always think of hope as grounded in the future. Wrong. Hope is always grounded in the past. Hope simply challenges us to remember, always, that we have survived everything in life to this point — and in even better shape often than we were when our troubles began. So why not this situation, too? Hope. You have no reason not to.

JOAN CHITTISTER
The Psalms

Hope

If the space within us feels desolate as a tomb, if the light has not yet dawned in the garden shadows, we are in good company. In such a place, Mary walked bewildered, and there she met the risen Christ. We who weep seek him too; tenderly he touches eyes blinded by tears.

KATHY COFFEY
Dancing in the Margins

Hope

Perhaps in the next hundred years we will come to think of the religions of the world as similar to one another as we today think the denominations of Christianity to be. That would be a major breakthrough in consciousness.

JOHN SHELBY SPONG
The Bishop's Voice

Humility

Humility and honesty are really the same thing . . .
The only honest response to life is a humble one.

RICHARD ROHR
Everything Belongs

Humility

The only wisdom we can hope to acquire
Is the wisdom of humility: humility is endless.

T. S. Eliot
Four Quartets

&

Humility means the courage to follow the road
that leads down into our very own reality;
into the shadow of our own self; and to take it
because it is the best way to reach God.

Anselm Gruen
Building Self-esteem

Humility

If you think you are not conceited, it means you are very conceited indeed.

C. S. LEWIS
The Joyful Christian

&

We all genuflect to someone, something. It may be our own ego, or money, or power, or prestige, or the God who made and sustains us. Humility places us in the arena of truth urging us to kneel and strike our breasts.

ROBERT F. MORNEAU
Ashes to Easter

Humility

*ohn of the Cross was convinced that an
authentic love of neighbor would be active in
the measure that humility and love of God were
present, for love of neighbor is the close companion
of humility.*

KIERAN KAVANAUGH
John of the Cross

*umility is the acceptance of our profound
ignorance with regard to God as well as so
many other things. We know what we know, and it
is not very much. We know what we do not know,
and that is a lot more.*

M. BASIL PENNINGTON
Lectio Divina

Humility

These virtues, humility and honesty, are the foundation of all spirituality, but they are hard won. Most of us have to crawl our way back to them.

RICHARD ROHR
Everything Belongs

&

It is therefore very important to understand that Christian humility implies not only a certain wise reserve in regard to one's own judgement — a good sense which sees that we are not always necessarily infallible in our ideas — but it also cherishes positive and trustful expectations of others.

THOMAS MERTON
Passion for Peace

Humility

Humble people are not people who belittle themselves, who shirk all the things they should do, because they do not trust themselves. They are not creeps who demean themselves by false obsequiousness. But they are people who have the courage to face the truth about themselves, and so to behave modestly.

ANSELM GRUEN
Angels of Grace

Humility

umility is the prerequisite for letting God be God, for developing a sense for God as the wholly other. The closer people come to God, the humbler they get. Then they can feel how far removed they are from God's holiness. Humility is the response to the experience of God.

ANSELM GRUEN
Heaven Begins Within You

"ever say 'never'" (i.e., "I would never. . . .") is a lesson often learned only after a long process of letting go and of "ego deflation," but it is essential for authentic humility and for the compassion that allows us to experience God.

BARBARA FIAND
Prayer and the Quest for Healing

Humility

Quite simply, piety is enhanced neither by individual or institutional certitude, nor by doctrinal obsession with correctness. It flows out of a humble heart emptied of all presuppositions, assumptions, and expectations.

BARBARA FIAND
Prayer and the Quest for Healing

&

Humility is not only related to humus, earth, but to humor. You need humor to accept yourself.

ANSELM GRUEN
Building Self-esteem

Intimacy

*T*he first lesson to be learned about intimacy and emotional involvement begins with an examination of our own needs. . . . Very often the biggest hurts, the ones that make us set up the highest defenses, arise precisely because we respond to ourselves more than to other persons.

EUGENE KENNEDY
The Pain of Being Human

Intimacy

*eresa of Avila uses the image of human friend-
ship to describe our intimacy with God, who
is indescribably close to us, intimately near, person-
ally and passionately present. This love startles us.
Most of us don't have the courage to embrace it.*

TESSA BIELECKI
Teresa of Avila

&

*ur love must have a double direction, one
pointing to the transcendent mystery of God
and the other to our sisters and brothers who are
the immanent mystery surrounding us.*

ROBERT F. MORNEAU
From Resurrection to Pentecost

Intimacy

he faces of intimacy are as diverse as stars, as unique as snowflakes. Pick up any book of portraits, any record of history, and you will see what I mean. Walk through any park on a summer's day and catch a couple in love smiling into each other's eyes.

SUSAN MUTO
Late Have I Loved Thee

ou do not resolve the God question in your head — or even in the perfection of moral response. It is resolved IN YOU, when you agree to bear the mystery of God: God's suffering for the world and God's ecstasy in the world. That is much harder, I'm afraid, than just trying to be "good."

RICHARD ROHR
Everything Belongs

Intimacy

nly in Christianity could the human being be called an intimate of God. This is true because in Christ God has become one of us, thereby establishing a parity totally beyond our capacity even to imagine or hope for.

ROBERT BARRON
Heaven in Stone and Glass

&

ndeed, there is only one reason for us to take up the challenge of relationship, but it is a compelling one — we must fully relate if we are to fully live.

STEVEN HARRISON
Being One

Intimacy

By watching carefully our endless desire to love, we come to the growing awareness that we can love only because we have been loved first, and that we can offer intimacy only because we are born out of the inner intimacy of God himself.

HENRI J. M. NOUWEN
Show Me the Way

&

The secret of happiness in life, that which finally gives it meaning and purpose, is to feel that someone is seeking You, longing for You, dreaming about You. In this respect, more than anything else, human lovers are sacraments for You.

ANDREW GREELEY
Windows

Intimacy

Intimacy is more than presence; it is a soul
connection, fully felt, mystical moments that
connect us to our selves, to others, to the universe
and the divine.

JAMES CONLON
The Sacred Impulse

&

When we enjoy God's nearness, prayer is like
play. Ours is a relationship of carefree aban-
donment to a beneficial mystery. It is as if God
bounces us in the air like children laughing. Worry
wanes. Fear fades. Joy abounds. Peace prevails. We
humans become fully alive. Such is the grace of
recovered intimacy.

SUSAN MUTO
Late Have I Loved Thee

Justice

In silence
We hear God's whisper
Moving like a feather
Through our being,
Stroking and transforming
Timid souls into
Fiery passion
For justice.

EDWINA GATELEY
A Mystical Heart

Justice

There is only one winner in war. The winner is not justice, not liberty, not Christian truth. The winner is war itself.

THOMAS MERTON
Passion for Peace

&

To the prophets a minor, commonplace sort of injustice assumes almost cosmic proportions.

ABRAHAM JOSHUA HESCHEL
I Asked for Wonder

Justice

*J*ustice and peace workers can strive to change
systems and standards of living, but they must
also endure seeing what disease and starvation does
to people before the systemic changes happen.

JOYCE RUPP
Your Sorrow Is My Sorrow

&

*W*ithin an evil world any commitment to
justice and love is deadly dangerous.

EDWARD SCHILLEBEECKX
Church

Justice

To those who suffer
so much from the oppression
of the powerful
be with me
I am ready
to be a servant
to be a friend
of the marginated
be with me.

MICHAEL KENNEDY
Eyes on the Cross

*T*he more one can directly associate with the victims of injustice, share their lot, plead their cause and defend them, the more one will grow spiritually.

BENEDICT J. GROESCHEL
Spiritual Passages

&

*A*ll people take a step into wholeness when they can affirm and live out openly and honestly the deepest identities of their lives.

JOHN SHELBY SPONG
The Bishop's Voice

Justice

We are called to demand of both church and society that the self, each of us, is to be accorded justice, acceptance, affirmation, and protection.

JOHN SHELBY SPONG
The Bishop's Voice

&

Liberating the oppressed, setting free those who are downtrodden, standing with them against oppressive systems, and radically changing our own conduct, our institutions and policies on behalf of justice — that is what walking the road to Galilee is all about. That is what believing in the resurrection means.

BARBARA FIAND
Prayer and the Quest for Healing

Justice

Since peace and justice are among the most powerful signs of the reign of God present in this world, it belongs to the essential mission of the church to make these realities more visible in our time, so marked by oppression, violence, injustice, and threat of total destruction.

ELIZABETH A. JOHNSON
Consider Jesus

&

Charity is about giving a hungry man some bread, while justice is about trying to change the system so that nobody has excess bread while some have none; charity is about treating your neighbors with respect, while justice is about trying to get at the deeper roots of racism.

RONALD ROLHEISER
The Holy Longing

Ministry

Stewardship of self is so inextricably bound up with stewardship of others, though, that being available to ourselves is never really possible if we are not also open and sensitive to other people.

ROBERT WICKS
Availability

Ministry

The task of each Christian today is to help defend and restore the basic human values without which grace and spirituality will have little practical meaning in the life of man.

THOMAS MERTON
Life and Holiness

&

Nobody lives happily ever after. We live happily when we live with a sense of purpose and when we are unafraid of living in a world in which things are seldom settled, few things are permanently improved, and where love does not take care of itself.

EUGENE KENNEDY
A Sense of Life, A Sense of Sin

Ministry

No one has a more solemn obligation to understand the true nature of man's predicament than he who is called to a life of special holiness and dedication. The priest, the religious, the lay leader must, whether he likes it or not, fulfill in the world the role of a prophet.

THOMAS MERTON
Passion for Peace

&

To bring the gospel to all the needy in the world, not only through words but through solidarity in action ... is the very nature of Christianity.

EDWARD SCHILLEBEECKX
Church

Ministry

*R*emember that we have little evidence that
Jesus spent a lot of time in church.

JOAN CHITTISTER
The Psalms

&

*T*oday we are making an effort to lift women
from anonymity to visibility, from the margins
to the center.

MIRIAM THERESE WINTER
The Gospel According to Mary

Ministry

I t could well be that we are God's agent to make present to this person, this meeting, this wake service the very presence of Christ. What a noble mission, what a serious responsibility, what a happy calling.

ROBERT F. MORNEAU
From Resurrection to Pentecost

I do not know what's happened to my life. I did not lead a life; I worked, wrote, taught, tried to do my duty and earn my living. I tried in this ordinary everyday way to serve God — that's it.
— *Karl Rahner*

ROBERT ELLSBERG
All Saints

Ministry

ands, do what you're bid:
Bring the balloons of the mind
That belies and drags in the wind
Into its narrow shed.

W. B. YEATS
The Balloons of the Mind (from Bartlett's Quotations)

od is hiding in the world.
Our task is to let the divine emerge from our
deeds.

ABRAHAM JOSHUA HESCHEL
I Asked for Wonder

Passion

Hatred is not the opposite of love: indifference is, just as spiritual indifference rather than atheism is the enemy of authentic religion.

DIARMUID O'MURCHÚ
Quantum Theology

*he beatitudes tell us to hunger and thirst
     after justice; but part of this hungering is
righteous anger against violence, whether military,
sexual, economic or ecological, the denial of human
rights, and the abuse of power within any institu-
tion, even the Church itself.*

MARY C. GREY
The Outrageous Pursuit of Hope

Passion

hose who live without passion lack bite, lack force, lack fullness of life.

ANSELM GRUEN
Angels of Grace

&

he image of the passionless Christian — the sweet, saccharin, flaccid, and passive partici-pant in life — is not worthy of the ideals of Chris-tianity. To know, for instance, that according to the U.S. Budget Office, welfare in all its forms is only 3 percent of the budget and not be angry about the ruthless political attack on the disadvantaged families that receive it in the wealthiest country in the world is to be less than Christian.

JOAN CHITTISTER
The Psalms

One must live as best one can with as much
vigor and hope and generosity as is available.
And above all with the sense that one is loved.
By You.

ANDREW GREELEY
Windows

&

I pray — for fashion's word is out
And prayer comes round again —
That I may seem, though I die old,
A foolish, passionate man.

W. B. YEATS
A Prayer for Old Age (from Bartlett's Quotations)

Passion

If an individual's feelings do not get stirred up in one way or another, then it is appropriate to wonder whether anything is going on in a helping relationship of which he or she is a part.

EUGENE KENNEDY
Free To Be Human

&

The prophet is a man who feels fiercely . . . God is raging in the prophet's words.

ABRAHAM JOSHUA HESCHEL
I Asked for Wonder

Passion

M uch of what empowered the early Christian community has suffered the calcification of time and needs to regain its passion.

BARBARA FIAND
Where Two or Three Are Gathered

&

P assion has to do with experience. If you suppress it, you lose experience. If you go with it, you experience the new, the unimagined.

ANSELM GRUEN
Angels of Grace

Passion

It is good news to know that Jesus is handed over to passion, and through his passion accomplishes his divine task on earth. It is good news for a world passionately searching for wholeness.

HENRI J. M. NOUWEN
Show Me the Way

Prayer

For Jesus, prayer seems to be a matter of waiting in love. Returning to love. Trusting that love is the bottom stream of reality. That's why prayer isn't primarily words; it's primarily a place, an attitude, a stance.

RICHARD ROHR
Everything Belongs

Prayer

One more prayer that is sure to be answered: often we beg God to take care of the people we love. We do not need to. God loves our loved ones more than we do.

ROBERT J. CORMIER
A Faith That Makes Sense

&

In the clumsy move
From prayer
To telephone,
I suddenly know
(though with less comfort)
that God
is in the ringing.

EDWINA GATELEY
A Mystical Heart

Prayer

*T*o pray without ceasing is to thank God for
promises fulfilled and hopes for what the
future holds.

SUSAN MUTO
Late Have I Loved Thee

&

*S*pirituality and prayer, however much they
invite us to solitude and silence, can only grow
and develop toward divine love in the one who is
open, giving, and vulnerable.

BENEDICT J. GROESCHEL
Spiritual Passages

Prayer

Prayer without words is not so much expressing our dependence on God as experiencing it and being so overwhelmed by that experience that words become so inadequate that they are useless. Nor are they really needed. Silence alone is appropriate.

WILLIAM SHANNON
Silence on Fire

&

Prayer is the movement from illusion to reality. It's less about changing God's mind than about embracing the reality of our own lives.

JAMES CONLON
The Sacred Impulse

Prayer

Sweet hour of prayer, sweet hour of prayer,
That calls me from a world of care,
And bids me at my Father's throne,
Make all my wants and wishes known!
In seasons of distress and grief,
My soul has often found relief,
And often escaped the tempter's snare
By your return, sweet hour of prayer.
— William W. Walford (adapted)

PHYLLIS TICKLE
The Divine Hours

Prayer

he Rosary is both a contemplative and healing prayer. The mysteries of Christ become the focus of our contemplation; as we offer our whole life to God in union with Mary, in the context of the mysteries of her Son, we experience peace and healing, forgiveness and reconciliation.

JIM MCMANUS
All Generations Will Call Me Blessed

Prayer

What if prayer flowed in us very much as our blood does — as a constant "yes" to life and to love, a perpetual affirmation and surrender — not anything we do but rather everything we are?

BARBARA FIAND
Prayer and the Quest for Healing

Prayer

If we go to prayer looking for or expecting an experience of some sort, to find peace or quiet, if we are concerned about doing it right, getting the right effect or result, then we are no longer seeking God. We are in some way seeking ourselves, seeking something for ourselves, and we cannot simply be to God.

M. BASIL PENNINGTON
Centering Prayer

Prayer

There is probably nothing more truly radical than real persons of prayer because they are beholden to no ideology or economic system, but only to God.

RICHARD ROHR
Everything Belongs

The Angelus, in popular language, is above all the resounding call that comes from our belfries three times a day and, more than simply a call, it represents prayer itself. The prayer is unimaginable without the ringing that introduces it. By contrast, it is easy to imagine it the other way around: that is, only the ringing.

JEAN FOURNÉE
Praying the Angelus

Solitude

*T*he "wilderness" of man's spirit is not yet totally hostile to all spiritual life. On the contrary, its silence is still a healing silence.

THOMAS MERTON
Passion for Peace

*O*nly when we have the absolute contentment
of aloneness can we give expression to love. This
is our purification.

STEVEN HARRISON
Being One

&

*N*ot all men are called to be hermits, but all
men need enough silence and solitude in their
lives to enable the deep inner voice of their own
true self to be heard at least occasionally.

THOMAS MERTON
The Silent Life

Solitude

*I*t is as if I were the only man on the globe
And God, too, were alone,
Waiting for me.

ABRAHAM JOSHUA HESCHEL
I Asked for Wonder

&

*D*on't be afraid to be lonely. Loneliness teaches us
what we lack — and what we don't. Loneliness is a short course in personal development.

JOAN CHITTISTER
The Psalms

Solitude

When I enter that stillness inside my being, a feeling of freedom and trust grows in me. This is no mere outward show of self-confidence, constructed for the world to see, but an assurance derived from true inner freedom.

ANSELM GRUEN
Building Self-esteem

&

One of the casualties of modern living is the decline of solitude. . . . Even so, the sacrifice of solitude is particularly regrettable because solitude is a vital catalyst for creativity and a source for healing during periods of loss.

CHARLES M. SHELTON
Achieving Moral Health

Solitude

Prayerful solitude with God makes it possible
for us to be with others and to deal intimately
even with those in pain.

ROBERT WICKS
Availability

&

Once we have found the center of our life in our
own heart and have accepted our aloneness,
not as a fate but as a vocation, we are able to offer
freedom to others. Once we have given up our desire
to be fully fulfilled, we can offer emptiness to others.

HENRI J. M. NOUWEN
Show Me the Way

Solitude

loneness is the path to who we are: nothing but space for what is here and now and what may be. Giving up the illusion that others make us whole, we gain a sense of wholeness in our solitude. We notice both our space and our boundaries.

DAVID RICHO
Catholic Means Universal

&

n the tempestuous ocean of time and toil there are islands of stillness where man can enter a harbor and reclaim his dignity. The island is the seventh day, the Sabbath, a day of detachment from things, instruments and practical affairs as well as of attachment to the spirit.

ABRAHAM JOSHUA HESCHEL
I Asked for Wonder

Solitude

In my loneliness I discover my own depths, the ground of my being, and in these depths I am deeply connected with all human beings. There I feel that, as Ovid said, nothing human is alien to me, that in my inmost self I am connected with all other people.

ANSELM GRUEN
Angels of Grace

&

To enter the space of our solitude is to find ourselves in a mysterious way in solidarity with all seekers.

SUSAN MUTO
Late Have I Loved Thee

oman are only now discovering the value of their intuition, the necessity for solitude (for which they have longed), and the need to trust what they experience as sacred in their lives, whether this be through relationships or nature or other meaningful sources.

JOYCE RUPP
Dear Heart, Come Home

Spirituality

Spirituality is about seeing. It's not about earning or achieving. It's about relationships rather than results or requirements. Once you see, the rest follows. You don't need to push the river, because you are in it.

RICHARD ROHR
Everything Belongs

The spiritual crisis, when it visits our lives, is the moment of profound change. It is the moment when we may come to the root of our pain, the source of our existential dilemma. We do not need to fix it, we do not need to run from it, we do not need to fear it. We do not need to do anything. In doing nothing, we are left with an acute awareness of all that is occurring. An acute awareness of all that is occurring is, after all, what we are.

STEVEN HARRISON
Being One

Spirituality

To truly see, to find You and Your spirit where You lurk in my house, I must listen more, and that can't be an act of the will either. Rather it has to be an act of letting go.

ANDREW GREELEY
Windows

&

Saintliness means living without division between word and action. If I would truly live in my own life the word I am speaking, my spoken words would become action, and miracles would happen whenever I opened my mouth.

HENRI J. M. NOUWEN
Show Me the Way

Spirituality

For the early monks spiritual life also meant the art of healthy living. . . . Nowadays we could surely never imitate the lifestyle of the old monks. But the basic principle that order outside leads to order inside, that a healthy way of living also makes the soul healthy, is something we can still live today.

ANSELM GRUEN
Heaven Begins Within You

&

My task as a Christian and indeed as a human being is to accept reality in its fullness. This means accepting the fact that my spirituality encompasses my total existence, not just a part of it.

WILLIAM SHANNON
Silence on Fire

Spirituality

pirituality is not just about religion, or church attendance, or fidelity to one or other legal requirement. Spirituality is understood to be an innate wisdom of the human heart that enlivens a zest for life, a search for meaning and purpose, a love for all that is good and beautiful, a passion to create a better world, a sensitivity to the life-energy (God, if you wish) that permeates the entire cosmos.

DIARMUID O' MURCHÚ
Our World in Transition

149

Spirituality

he spiritual life is less about breaking out of the self to build a bridge to You, and more about recognizing You present in the self, the Spirit talking to our spirit as St. Paul put it.

ANDREW GREELEY
Windows

&

ong before we do anything explicitly religious at all, we have to do something about the fire that burns within us. What we do with that fire, how we channel it, is our spirituality. Thus, we all have a spirituality whether we want one or not, whether we are religious or not.

RONALD ROLHEISER
The Holy Longing

Spirituality

For those of us exploring Christian spirituality, whether for the first time or as we deepen our spiritual understandings, we can use the computer as a place to try on new words and new understandings within the confines of a supportive Christian community. Once we feel that we have found what we need, we can begin to take these new realities into our daily lives beyond the computer screen.

Debra K. Farrington
Romancing the Holy

ernard of Clairvaux struggled to live a good
Christian life, just as all of us do. Maybe that
is what makes him attractive as a spiritual guide.
His spiritual insights are not detached observations
but are the fruit of a life of intense engagement
with God and with other human beings.

DENNIS E. TAMBURELLO
Bernard of Clairvaux

Spirituality

To affirm the truth of a unique Christian spirituality is not to belittle in any way the spiritual roads discovered by the mystics of non-biblical religions; nor is it to denigrate the ways of religious philosophies, still less to disparage the insights of Islamic and Jewish spirituality. It is not difficult for the believing Catholic to see everywhere in these movements the operation of grace.

BENEDICT J. GROESCHEL
Spiritual Passages

e participate in the life of the local church community, not to take refuge from daily living, but to be schooled in the graced pattern of Christian living and sent out with a renewed sense of divine presence and a renewed recognition of the way of life that the gospel demands of us. In this school of discipleship we discover ourselves in a new way.

RICHARD R. GAILLARDETZ
Transforming Our Days

Spirituality

piritual apartheid is very dangerous for our spiritual health, for it tends to limit spirituality; restricting it to certain "holy" places and "sacred" times. This type of spirituality enshrines a mentality that would think that I am "spiritual" only on certain occasions and that most of the time I am not.

WILLIAM SHANNON
Silence on Fire

&

e're creatures of meaning and the drive toward meaning comes from deep within — not just within ourselves, but also, I dare to suggest, from deep within creation itself.

DIARMUID O' MURCHÚ
Quantum Theology

Suffering

ary met the bloodied and disfigured Seed of
her womb with great tenderness and love.
Something in us refuses to do this. We tend to move
away from, rather than toward, what hurts us. We
choose to disconnect from it rather than to approach
our suffering with compassion and care.

JOYCE RUPP
Your Sorrow Is My Sorrow

Suffering

ere's the interesting, the tough, the beautiful truth: joy and sorrow come from the same place. It is only what we love, in other words, that can really make us suffer. So if you want to know from where your hard spots in life will come, just ask yourself what you really love the most. Be honest: REALLY love. It's there in that place alone where loss and lesson wait.

JOAN CHITTISTER
The Psalms

Suffering

uffering is a dreadful teacher but often the beginning of the best in us. Suffering and creativity are often interdependent. Pain produces a terrible tension released in our creative response. Suffering can be like a grain of sand in an oyster: it can create a magnificent pearl.

TESSA BIELECKI
Teresa of Avila

Suffering

Perhaps one of the starkest portraits of (an) abandoned state is that of Mary Magdalene outside the tomb: alone, weeping, confused, disoriented. If we recognize something of ourselves in her, or have known the seeming futility of her vigil there, then we can sense a little of the emptiness she must feel.

KATHY COFFEY
Dancing in the Margins

Suffering

If bad things did not hurt, good things would not be giving us a glimpse of heaven. And if some things were not monstrous, we could not know how wonderful is the good, and how great that we have achieved it.

ROBERT J. CORMIER
A Faith That Makes Sense

&

One of the toughest things in life is to walk the journey of intense suffering of someone who is dear to us. Mary knew this when she encountered the tattered remnant of her Child on the road to his death.

JOYCE RUPP
Your Sorrow Is My Sorrow

Suffering

We discovered your mercy only when we realized that You suffered, and suffer with us, and that Good Friday is the revelation of that suffering.

ANDREW GREELEY
Windows

&

Neither revolutions nor faith is won without keen suffering. For me Christ was not to be bought for thirty pieces of silver but with my heart's blood. We buy not cheap in this market.
— Dorothy Day

ROBERT ELLSBERG
All Saints

161

Suffering

*E*ntering into the suffering of the poor is the way to become obedient, that is, a listener to God. Suffering accepted and shared in love breaks down our selfish defenses and sets us free to accept God's guidance.

HENRI J. M. NOUWEN
Show Me the Way

&

*S*uffering is a mysterious and inescapable part of life — recognized or repressed, embraced or resisted. Grappling creatively with suffering, especially physical and emotional pain, is what we mean by "embracing the cross."

TESSA BIELECKI
Teresa of Avila

Suffering

*A*pathy, at its root, refers to the inability to suffer. It is present wherever in our culture there are people so obsessed with avoiding inconvenience, pain, or suffering that they end up avoiding all human relationships that might require risk and vulnerability.

RICHARD R. GAILLARDETZ
Transforming Our Days

Suffering

Spiritual maturity is a mystery. To be sure, grace builds on nature. It helps if we receive from God the gift of good parents, solid friendships, supportive peers. Love received increases our capacity to love in return. But grace can also form us into mature Christians through suffering.

SUSAN MUTO
Late Have I Loved Thee

Suffering

I do not believe that death at age 29 from leukemia or at age 26 in an automobile accident is an expression of God's will. Surely God desires life, health, and wholeness for those created in this God's image. The religious answers we have devised through the ages to defend God in the face of human tragedy seem to me to fail miserably.

JOHN SHELBY SPONG
The Bishop's Voice

Suffering

S uffering, therefore, is a sign of faith and depth, and even life. And no one wants to be less alive. Moreover, once we recognize that suffering reflects our glimpse of how things will be, what caused us pain can bring us joy.

ROBERT J. CORMIER
A Faith That Makes Sense

&

I nstead of declaring anything and everything to be the will of God, we must be willing to ask ourselves where in the midst of our pains and sufferings we can discern the loving presence of God.

HENRI J. M. NOUWEN
Show Me the Way

Suffering

$\mathcal{S}$uffering people are the privileged place where
the God of compassion is to be found.

ELIZABETH A. JOHNSON
Consider Jesus

&

$\mathcal{T}$he deep truth is that our human suffering
need not be an obstacle to the joy and peace
we so desire, but can become, instead, the means
to it.

HENRI J. M. NOUWEN
Life of the Beloved

Suffering

uffering is what tempers the arrogance of youth and turns us into men and women who finally know that to be finite, to be vulnerable, to be weak is not to be a failure. It is to be human.

JOAN CHITTISTER
The Psalms

&

o seek suffering for its own sake is dysfunctional. Enough pain enters everyone's life unsought. But to seek an understanding of pain in the cross of Christ has helped people for many years. Christians come to the cross not to seek suffering, but to find Christ. At all times and in all situations, he is our center and hope.

KATHY COFFEY
Dancing in the Margins

Vocation

hat usually attracts young people to a life of deeply committed faith or even to a religious vocation is more often than not the humanity of someone who is already in that life.

ELIZABETH A. JOHNSON
Consider Jesus

*S*ometimes, however, to be a "ruined man" is itself a vocation.

T. S. ELIOT
"East Coker" from Four Quartets
from Collected Poems 1909–1962

&

*O*ur real journey in life is interior: it is a matter of growth, deepening, and of an ever greater surrender to the creative action of love and grace in our hearts.

THOMAS MERTON
The Asian Journal of Thomas Merton

Vocation

Bit by intelligible bit, a vocation lets us express our healthiest instincts, our noblest desires. We commit to goals well beyond ourselves—beauty, tenacity, compassion. Or perhaps we cut back. Doing less is often heroic, and that choice also blesses us. In small things and in large, we can attend to the haunting inner summons of our soul.

MARSHA SINETAR
Holy Work

herever we see real service we also see joy, because in the midst of service a divine presence becomes visible and a gift is offered.

HENRI J. M. NOUWEN
Show Me the Way

&

eing simply ourselves (and being that as perfectly as possible) is enough, is our vocation — the holy work we are, a mission rich enough to produce a lifetime of reward.

MARSHA SINETAR
Holy Work

Vocation

An authentic call cannot be based on the abolition of the "true self." It cannot be based on conformity to the ideals and examples of others. Although we admire Martin Luther King, Jr., Mahatma Ghandi, Dorothy Day, Oscar Romero and others, our true calling will not be discovered through imitating them or anyone else.

JAMES CONLON
The Sacred Impulse

Vocation

hatever happens to me in life
I must believe that somewhere
In the mess or madness of it all,
There is a sacred potential —
A possibility for wondrous redemption
In the embracing of all that is.

EDWINA GATELEY
A Mystical Heart

eligious life is not primarily about religion.
By restricting it to a religious context, we
violate the very essence of our global and cultural
outreach. We set limitations, restrictions, and even
barriers to what we are meant to be about.

DIARMUID O' MURCHÚ
Poverty, Celibacy and Obedience

Vocation

his is vocation: that we answer God's call to be and to give of ourselves, in service. That we honor Life intentionally through some line of natural, concrete endeavor: be it bricklaying or basket weaving. The form of work makes no difference. Later, we may be equipped for more.

MARSHA SINETAR
Holy Work

Vocation

f I never become what I am meant to be, but always remain what I am not, I shall spend eternity contradicting myself by being at once something and nothing, a life that wants to live and is dead, and a death that wants to be dead and cannot quite achieve its own death because it still has to exist.

JAMES CONLON
The Sacred Impulse

Vocation

he universal call and vocation of us all is a call to holiness, the perfection of charity. Our lives are to be lives of service, like the life of Jesus. To fulfill that calling, we need to experience the Spirit who enlightens, enkindles, and enables us to discern and do God's will.

ROBERT F. MORNEAU
Ashes to Easter

Vocation

As a Christian, I am called to become bread for the world: bread that is taken, blessed, broken and given. Most importantly, however, (these four words) summarize my life as a human being because in every moment of my life somewhere, somehow the taking, the blessing, the breaking and the giving are happening

HENRI J. M. NOUWEN
Life of the Beloved

Acknowledgments

We wish to acknowledge the following publishers and authors for permission to reprint previously published material.

From *Achieving Moral Health* by Charles M. Shelton Ph.D. Copyright © 2000 by Charles M. Shelton. Reprinted by permission of the Crossroad Publishing Company.

From *All Generations Will Call Me Blessed* by Jim McManus, C.Ss.R. Copyright © 1999 by Jim McManus, C.Ss.R. Reprinted by permission of the Crossroad Publishing Company.

From *All Saints* by Robert Ellsberg. Copyright © 1997 by Robert Ellsberg. Reprinted by permission of the Crossroad Publishing Company.

From *Angels of Grace* by Anselm Gruen. English translation copyright © 1998 Burns & Oates/Search Press Limited. Reprinted by permission of the Crossroad Publishing Company. UK/Commonwealth rights, reprinted by permission of Burns & Oates, Kent, England.

From *Ashes to Easter* by Robert F. Morneau. Copyright © 1996 by Robert F. Morneau. Reprinted by permission of the Crossroad Publishing Company.

From *The Asian Journals of Thomas Merton* by Thomas Merton, copyright © 1975 by The Trustees of the Merton Legacy Trust. Reprinted by permission of New Directions Publishing Corp.

From *Being One: Finding Oneself in Relationship* by Steven Harrison. Copyright © 1999 by Steven Harrison. Reprinted by permission of the Crossroad Publishing Company.

From *Bernard of Clairvaux* by Dennis Tamburello. Copyright © 2000 by Dennis Tamburello, O.F.M. Reprinted by permission of the Crossroad Publishing Company.

From *Beyond the Mirror* by Henri J. M. Nouwen. Copyright © 1990 by Henri J. M. Nouwen. Reprinted by permission of the Crossroad Publishing Company.

From *The Bishop's Voice* by John Shelby Spong. Copyright © 1999 by John Shelby Spong and Christine M. Spong. Reprinted by permission of the Crossroad Publishing Company.

179

Acknowledgments

From *Building Self-Esteem* by Anselm Gruen. English translation copyright © 2000 Burns & Oates/Search Press Limited. Reprinted by permission of the Crossroad Publishing Company. UK/Commonwealth rights, reprinted by permission of Burns & Oates, Kent England.

From *Catholic Means Universal* by David Richo, Ph.D. Copyright © 2000 by David Richo. Reprinted by permission of the Crossroad Publishing Company.

From *Centering Prayer* by M. Basil Pennington. Reprinted by permission of Doubleday, a Division of Random House, Inc.

From *Church* by Edward Schillebeeckx. Copyright © 1989 by Uitgeverij H. Nelissen. English translation copyright © 1990 by the Crossroad Publishing Company. Reprinted by permission of the Crossroad Publishing Company.

From *Consider Jesus* by Elizabeth Johnson. Copyright © 1990 by Elizabeth Johnson. Reprinted by permission of the Crossroad Publishing Company.

From *Dancing in the Margins* by Kathy Coffey. Copyright © 1999 by Kathy Coffey. Reprinted by permission of the Crossroad Publishing Company.

From *Dear Heart, Come Home: The Path of Midlife Spirituality* by Joyce Rupp. Copyright © 1996 by Joyce Rupp. Reprinted by permission of the Crossroad Publishing Company.

From *The Divine Hours* edited by Phyllis Tickle. Reprinted by permission of the author.

From "East Coker" from *Four Quartets* from *Collected Poems 1909-1962* by T. S. Eliot. Reprinted in the United States by permission of Harcourt, Inc. and UK/Commonwealth permission by Faber and Faber, England.

From *Everybody Has an Angel* by Anselm Gruen. English translation copyright © 2000 by the Crossroad Publishing Company. Reprinted by permission of the Crossroad Publishing Company.

From *Everything Belongs* by Richard Rohr. Copyright © 1999 by Richard Rohr. Reprinted by permission of the Crossroad Publishing Company.

From *Eyes on the Cross* by Michael Kennedy. Copyright © 2001 by Michael Kennedy. Reprinted by permission of the Crossroad Publishing Company.

From *Eyes on Jesus* by Michael Kennedy. Copyright © 1999 by Michael Kennedy. Reprinted by permission of the Crossroad Publishing Company.

From *A Faith That Makes Sense* by Robert J. Cormier. Copyright © 1999 by Robert J. Cormier. Reprinted by permission of the Crossroad Publishing Company.

Acknowledgments

From *Free To Be Human* by Eugene Kennedy. Copyright © 1987 by Eugene Kennedy. Reprinted by permission of Doubleday, a Division of Random House, Inc.

From *The Gospel According to Mary* by Miriam Therese Winter. Copyright © 1993 by the Medical Missionary Sisters. Reprinted by permission of the Crossroad Publishing Company.

From *Heaven Begins Within You* by Anselm Gruen. English translation copyright © 1999 by the Crossroad Publishing Company. Reprinted by permission of the Crossroad Publishing Company.

From *Heaven in Stone and Glass* by Robert Barron. Copyright © 2000 by Robert Barron. Reprinted by permission of the Crossroad Publishing Company.

From *Here and Now* by Henri J. M. Nouwen. Copyright © 1994 by Henri J. M. Nouwen. Reprinted by permission of the Crossroad Publishing Company.

From *The Holy Longing* by Ronald Rolheiser. Reprinted by permission of Doubleday, a Division of Random House, Inc.

From *Holy Work* by Marsha Sinetar. Copyright © 1998 by Sinetar & Associates. Reprinted by permission of the Crossroad Publishing Company.

From *I Asked for Wonder* by Abraham Joshua Heschel edited by Samuel H. Dresner. Copyright © 1983 by Samuel H. Dresner. Reprinted by permission of the Crossroad Publishing Company.

From *Job and the Mystery of Suffering* by Richard Rohr. Copyright © 1996 by Richard Rohr. Reprinted by permission of the Crossroad Publishing Company.

From *John of the Cross* by Kieran Kavanagh. Copyright © 1999 by the Washington Province of Discalced Carmelite Friars. Inc. Reprinted by permission of the Crossroad Publishing Company.

From *The Joyful Christian* by C.S. Lewis. Copyright © 1977 by C.S. Lewis Pty. Ltd. Extract printed by permission.

From *Late Have I Loved Thee: The Recovery of Intimacy* by Susan Muto. Copyright © 1995 by Susan Muto. Reprinted by permission of the Crossroad Publishing Company.

From *Lectio Divina* by M. Basil Pennington. Copyright © 1998 by the Cistercian Abbey of Spencer, Inc. Reprinted by permission of the Crossroad Publishing Company.

Acknowledgments

From *Life of the Beloved* by Henri J. M. Nouwen. Copyright © 1992 by Henri J. M. Nouwen. Reprinted by permission of the Crossroad Publishing Company.

From *Life and Holiness* by Thomas Merton. Copyright © 1969 by the Trustees of the Thomas Merton Legacy Trust. Reprinted by permission of Doubleday, a Division of Random House, Inc.

From *A Listening Heart* by David Steindl-Rast. Copyright © 1983, 1999 by David Steindl-Rast. Reprinted by permission of the Crossroad Publishing Company.

From *A Mystical Heart* by Edwina Gateley. Copyright © 1998 by Edwina Gateley. Reprinted by permission of the Crossroad Publishing Company.

From *101 Ways to Nourish Your Soul* by Mitch Finley. Copyright ©1996 by Mitch Finley. Reprinted by permission of the Crossroad Publishing Company.

From *Our World in Transition* by Diarmuid O'Murchú. Copyright © 1992, 1995 by Diarmuid O'Murchú. Reprinted by permission of the Crossroad Publishing Company. UK/Commonwealth rights, reprinted by permission of the Book Guild, England.

From *The Outrageous Pursuit of Hope* by Mary C. Grey. Copyright © 2001 by Mary C. Grey. Reprinted by permission of the Crossroad Publishing Company. UK/Commonwealth rights, reprinted by permission of Darton Longman and Todd Ltd., London.

From *Passion for Peace: The Social Essays* by Thomas Merton, William Shannon (editor). Copyright © 1995 by The Trustees of the Merton Legacy Trust. Reprinted by permission of the Crossroad Publishing Company.

From *Poverty, Celibacy, and Obedience* by Diarmuid O'Murchú. Copyright © 1999 by Diarmuid O'Murchú, M.S.C. Reprinted by permission of the Crossroad Publishing Company.

From *Praying the Angelus* by Jean Fournée. English translation and supplement of the original French edition copyright © 2000 by the Crossroad Publishing Company. Reprinted by permission of the Crossroad Publishing Company.

From *Prayer and the Quest for Healing: Our Personal Transformation and Cosmic Responsibility* by Barbara Fiand. Copyright © 1999 by Barbara Fiand. Reprinted with permission of the Crossroad Publishing Company.

From *The Psalms* by Joan Chittister. Copyright © 1996 by Joan D. Chittister, O.S.B. Reprinted by permission of the Crossroad Publishing Company.

Acknowledgments

From *Quantum Theology* by Diarmuid O'Murchú. Copyright © 1997 by Diarmuid O'Murchú, M.S.C. Reprinted by permission of the Crossroad Publishing Company.

From *Restoring Relationships: Five Things to Try Before Saying Goodbye* by Peter M. Kalellis. Copyright © 2001 by Peter M. Kalellis. Reprinted by permission of the Crossroad Publishing Company.

From *Resurrection to Pentecost* by Robert F. Morneau. Copyright © 2000 by Robert F. Morneau. Reprinted by permission of the Crossroad Publishing Company.

From *Romancing the Holy* by Debra K. Farrington. Copyright © 1997 by Debra K. Farrington. Reprinted by permission of the Crossroad Publishing Company.

From *Sabbatical Journey* by Henri J. M. Nouwen. Copyright © 1998 by the Estate of Henri J. M. Nouwen. Reprinted by permission of the Crossroad Publishing Company.

From *The Sacred Impulse* by James Conlon. Copyright © 2001 by James Conlon. Reprinted by permission of the Crossroad Publishing Company.

From *A Sense of Life, A Sense of Sin* by Eugene Kennedy. Reprinted by permission of Doubleday, a Division of Random House, Inc.

From *Show Me the Way* by Henri J. M. Nouwen. This arrangement copyright © 1992 by Henri J. M. Nouwen. Reprinted by permission of the Crossroad Publishing Company.

From *Silence on Fire* by William Shannon. Copyright © 1991 by William Shannon. Reprinted by permission of the Crossroad Publishing Company.

From *The Silent Life* by Thomas Merton. Copyright © 1957 by the Abbey of Our Lady of Gethsemani. Reprinted by permission of Farrar, Straus & Giroux.

From *Simplicity* by Richard Rohr. English translation copyright © 1991 by the Crossroad Publishing Company. Reprinted by permission of the Crossroad Publishing Company.

From *Solanus Casey* by Michael Crosby, O.F.M. Cap. Copyright © 2000 by Michael Crosby O.F.M. Reprinted by permission of the Crossroad Publishing Company.

From *Spiritual Passages* by Benedict J. Groeschel. Copyright © 1983 by Benedict J. Groeschel. Reprinted by permission of the Crossroad Publishing Company.

Acknowledgments

From *Teresa of Avila* by Tessa Bielecki. Copyright © 1994 by Tessa Bielecki. Reprinted by permission of the Crossroad Publishing Company.

From *Transforming Our Days* by Richard R. Gaillardetz. Copyright © 2000 by Richard R. Gaillardetz. Reprinted by permission of the Crossroad Publishing Company.

From *The Use of Poetry and the Use of Criticism* by T.S. Eliot. Reprinted by permission of Faber and Faber, England.

From *What Does Christ Want?* by Bernard Häring. Copyright © 1992 by Bernard Häring. Reprinted by permission of the Society of St. Paul.

From *Where Two or Three Are Gathered* by Barbara Fiand. Copyright © 1992 by Barbara Fiand. Reprinted by permission of the Crossroad Publishing Company.

From *Windows: A Prayer Journal* by Andrew Greeley. Copyright © 1994 by Andrew M. Greeley. Reprinted by permission of the Crossroad Publishing Company.

From *With All Our Heart and Mind* by Sidney Callahan. Copyright © 1988 by Sidney Callahan. Reprinted by permission of the Crossroad Publishing Company.

From *Written That You May Believe* by Sandra M. Schneiders. Copyright © 1999 by Sandra M. Schneiders. Reprinted by permission of the Crossroad Publishing Company.

From *Your Sorrow Is My Sorrow* by Joyce Rupp. Copyright © 1999 by Joyce Rupp. Reprinted by permission of the Crossroad Publishing Company.